Picture Book Factory

by Murray Suid • illustrated by Mike Artell

Publisher: Roberta Suid
Editor: Carol Whiteley
Production: Susan Pinkerton

Related writing books from Monday Morning Books, Inc: *Book Factory, Writing Hangups, Greeting Cards, Write Through the Year, For the Love of Editing, For the Love of Letter Writing, For the Love of Research, For the Love of Stories.*

monday morning®

Monday Morning is a registered trademark of
Monday Morning Books, Inc.

ISBN 1-878279-16-5

Printed in the United States of America
9 8 7 6 5 4 3 2 1

CONTENTS

INTRODUCTION

Writing a children's picture book is not child's play. It requires at least as much imagination and careful thought as any other type of writing.

Here, the focus is on quality, not quantity. A finished picture book may have only a few hundred words. That's why each word must do its job. No wonder some of the era's best prose and poetry comes from the minds of writers such as Maurice Sendak and Margaret Wise Brown.

Few other formats provide greater challenges for blending text and art in ways that teach or stretch the imagination. Or both.

A WHOLLY WHOLE-LANGUAGE EXPERIENCE

The *Picture Book Factory* offers duplicatable lessons for creating dozens of different kinds of picture books—everything from the classic storybook to concept primers. The wide range of book types will enable young authors—working independently or cooperatively—to sharpen a variety of skills including describing, explaining, narrating, and convincing. It will also permit them to tap knowledge from inside and outside the curriculum—science, art, health, current events, math, and even manners. Older children can write for younger children, and younger children can write for each other.

While some students exhibit a knack for producing authentic-looking picture books, most will need careful teaching to handle this challenging format.

The starting point, as with most kinds of writing instruction, is reading. For children to write good picture books, they must know picture books from the inside out. Therefore, a list of model picture books provides examples that match most project categories.

Backing up the models are ready-to-use, detailed directions for each assignment. Before beginning the projects, however, you may wish to teach the key fundamentals of drafting, editing, illustrating, binding, and so on. Turn to the resource section "Becoming a Picture Book Author in Twelve Easy Steps."

Combine the twelve steps with the projects and you will be able to tap the creativity inside every child.

ACTIVITY BOOK

These days, many people worry that children spend too much time watching TV. An activity book can offer other things to do.

You can make costumes out of old rags and put on a play.

DIRECTIONS:
1. Brainstorm activities that children might try, for example, baking, dancing, dressing up, gardening, making music (singing, beating a drum), painting, playing games, creating clay figures, putting on a play or party, and so on.
2. Choose the focus for the book. It could be one kind of activity such as cooking, or a mixture of activities such as those for a rainy day.
3. Decide how to present the information. For example, a rainy day book might take the form of a story about two little kids who can't think of anything to do until they meet a character called the Fun Frog. Or the book might list ideas by place, for example, outdoors, indoors, and so on.
4. When writing the words, be sure to include important good behavior tips, for example, not to bang a drum loudly while other people are sleeping.

ADD-ON STORY

In an add-on story, something plus something plus something usually adds up to a surprise ending.

DIRECTIONS:
1. Brainstorm a list of places where people, animals, or things can get together, for example, an elevator, a tent, or a seesaw.
2. Pick one of the places and write a story about it. For example, two kids can be riding a seesaw when two others join, and then two more.
3. End the story with some sort of surprise, for example, the seesaw breaks because there are too many people riding on it.

"THAT LOOKS LIKE FUN," SAID ROSE.

"COME ON IN," SAID CARL.

"THAT LOOKS LIKE FUN," SAID FRANK.

"COME ON IN," THEY SAID.

Add-on Story Ideas

More and more people (or animals) are trying to:

    catch the same fish

    get on the same bus

    jump the same jump rope

    lie on the same beach blanket

    listen on the same telephone

    look in the same mirror

    paint on the same piece of paper

    play on the same jungle gym

    play the same piano

    read the same book

    ride in the same wagon

    ride on the same sled

    share the same cookie

    sit in the same chair

    smell the same flower

    squeeze through the same doorway

    stand under the same shade tree

    swim in the same pool or pond

ALPHABET BOOK

Getting to know and like letters is an important step in learning to read and love books.

DIRECTIONS:

1. Choose a focus for the book. Some alphabet books tie letters to just one subject, for example, animals or objects. Others include a variety of things.

2. Pick a style to use. Choices include:
   - one example for each letter (apple, banana, etc.)
   - several examples for each letter (apples, ants, arrows, ball, banana, bear)
   - same-letter sentences

3. Decide if the word for each letter will be given or if the reader will be asked to name the thing with the help of a picture clue, for example, "B is for_____" (on a page with a picture of a book).

4. Brainstorm, then choose the words.

5. Write the text and add the illustrations.

Variation: Illustrate letters not just at the beginning of a word but in the middle or at the end. For example, the "t" page might include train, water, and boat.

B is for

Catch the cute cats.

D
IS FOR DINOSAUR.

R is for

ANIMAL FACT BOOK

Most children are interested in all sorts of animals—
from tiny ants to giant dinosaurs.

DIRECTIONS:

1. Pick an animal to write about. It could be a cat, dog,
fish, or other household creature. Or it could be a worm,
a fly, a camel, or something even more unusual.
2. Collect plenty of interesting facts about the animal.
Read books or talk to an expert such as a zoo keeper.
3. Give careful thought to the organization of the book.
Simply listing facts may be boring. Think about
presenting the information in a story, for example, "A
Day in the Life of an Ant." Another idea is to include a
human character, for example, "Sandy Watches an Ant."
4. When writing the book, it's OK to use some big words,
but be sure to explain them. For example, in the
following paragraph, notice how "antennas" is explained:

> An ant can smell things even though it doesn't have
> a nose. Instead, it uses its antennas—little hair-like
> things that attach to its head.

5. Add an introduction that explains what's special
about the animal.

Variation: Write other beginning science books about
topics such as plants and seeds, rocks, stars, weather
(rain, snow, wind, and lightning).

ANIMAL STORYBOOK

From spiders to pigs—all kinds of animals have starred in children's books.

DIRECTIONS:
1. Pick one or more animals as the characters for a story.
2. List the most important actions of the main character. For example, a monkey chatters, swings, and eats bananas.
3. Think up a problem for the main character. Try to make the problem relate to something that kind of animal does. For example, a monkey's problem might be trying to find a place to swing from.
4. Before writing the story, decide whether or not to have the animal or animals talk.
5. Write the story, telling how the character deals with the problem.

Variation: Write a story in which the animal or animals act just like human beings.

There once was a worm who wanted to fly.

BABY BOOK

A book about babies can help children deal with the big changes that happen when a new family member arrives.

DIRECTIONS:
1. Decide the focus of the book. Topics include:
   - helping care for—and play with—the baby
   - dealing with emotions, for example, feeling left out of things
   - learning to enjoy having a baby in the family
2. Brainstorm a list of points to cover in the book. For example, a book about helping take care of a baby might include do's and don'ts.
3. Find information by reading and also by talking with experts such as doctors, preschool teachers, and friends who have babies in their homes.
4. Decide whether to present the information fact-by-fact or as a story that features a child or an animal, for example, "Betty Bear's New Brother."

Variation: Create a book *for* babies. Usually, this kind of book will have one big picture per page and only one or two words. Also, because babies give books rough treatment, the words and pictures should be pasted onto cardboard sheets that are then laminated.

BATH-TIME BOOK

A bathtub is more than just a place for getting clean. Mix a little imagination with the water and the soap, and the bathtub becomes a stage for all sorts of adventures.

DIRECTIONS:
1. Decide what kind of bath book to write. It might simply teach the reader how to get clean. Or it could be about having fun in the tub, overcoming fear of water, using the imagination, or all of the above.
2. Brainstorm a list of items that can be used when taking a bath—soap, towel, shampoo, plug, and—of course—water toys. Use these items in the story.
3. Decide what characters will appear in the book. In addition to the bather, there might be a parent, a pet, or a toy that comes to life.
4. After writing and illustrating the story, consider laminating the pages to make them waterproof. This way a reader could enjoy the book while taking a bath.

BEDTIME STORYBOOK

A calming book can help children get ready to enter dreamland.

DIRECTIONS:
1. List as many words as possible that relate to bedtime, for example, dream, pillow, rest, quiet, and warm milk.
2. Use the list to think up an idea for a book that will put children in the mood for going to sleep. The book can take the form of a story or it might just tell different things to do before falling asleep.
3. After writing the words, read them aloud and see if they have a gentle sound.
4. Illustrate the book with soft colors.

BODY BOOK

Fingernails, ear lobes, nostrils, belly button—the body is an interesting subject for children.

DIRECTIONS:
1. Choose a focus for the book. It's possible to write a book about a dozen parts of the body—or just one part, for example, the eyes.
2. Brainstorm points to cover. For example, a book about eyes might explain why there are two eyes, why eyes have different colors, what tears do, why some people wear glasses, and so on.
3. Collect information.
4. Decide how to present the facts. For example, a book about eyes might involve a trip to an eye doctor.
5. When writing the book, explain words that will be new to most readers.

Variation: Write a book that explains problems that affect the body, for example, rashes, sore throats, runny noses, and so on. Include tips on caring for the body.

COLOR BOOK

A book about colors can allow children to take pride in what they know about the world.

DIRECTIONS:
1. List things that can illustrate colors, for example:
    red—tomato, apple, traffic light
    blue—sky, eyes, water
    green—grass, money, beans
    purple—cabbage, grapes, African violets
2. Decide how to present the information. One way is to simply give information, for example, "An apple is red. The sky is blue." Another idea is to make the book into a guessing game in which an object is outlined on one page and the reader is asked to suggest the color, which appears on the next page. A third method is to tell a story about a child—or animal—learning to name the colors.
3. After writing and illustrating the book, include an introduction that explains why colors are important.

Variation: Write a silly color book. For example, show carrots that are blue and apples that are pink. On each page ask readers to say the real colors.

COMPARISON BOOK

People often must figure out how two things are alike and different. For example, shoppers do this when comparing items in a store. Scientists do it when studying things like plants. With the help of a good book, little children can learn this skill, too.

DIRECTIONS:
1. Pick two things to compare. Find things that will interest children, for example, a cat and a dog.
2. Brainstorm ways that the things are alike and the ways they are different. Think about how they look, how they are made, how they are used, their cost, their size, and so on. *Hint:* List the ways they are alike in one column and the ways they are different in another.
3. Write an introduction that explains why the two things are interesting.

Things to Compare

accordion and piano

airplane and bird

apartment and house

baseball and football

bath and shower

bicycle and skateboard

book and newspaper

bridge and tunnel

bus and train

camel and horse

candle and light bulb

car and truck

cat and lion

chair and sofa

elevator and escalator

eye and nose

foot and hand

fork and spoon

frown and smile

grapefruit and orange

ladder and stairs

moon and sun

ocean and river

painting and photograph

radio and television

refrigerator and stove

square and circle

summer and winter

triangle and square

COUNTING BOOK

Learning about numbers is important for every child. It can also be a lot of fun.

DIRECTIONS:
1. Decide how many numbers to include in the book. Most counting books go from one (or zero) to ten.
2. Brainstorm real things that can be used to illustrate each number. For example, items that illustrate "four" include: table (four legs), horse (four legs), and car (four wheels).
3. Design and create the pages. Will each number be written both as a word ("four") and in digit form ("4")? Will the number be placed above or below the thing? Will there also be "counting dots," circles that the reader can count? Will there be writing, for example, a rhyme that goes with the number:

> On this page, you can see
> The next number, which is three.

Variation: Some counting books use one type of thing, for example, monkeys. To add interest, objects appear in unusual places, for example, one monkey in a car, two monkeys in a plane, three in a boat, and so on.

EMOTIONS BOOK

Of all the subjects that children need to learn about, the most important may be what's inside them—their emotions.

DIRECTIONS:

1. Choose a topic for the book. It could be a single emotion or several, for example, love, hate, fear, envy, anger, and happiness. Or it might even be about the fact that people have emotions—whereas objects (like tables) don't.

2. Brainstorm ideas that relate to the emotion. For example, fear might suggest nightmares, scary movies, tears, and so on.

3. Learn as much as possible about the emotion—by reading and by talking with people.

4. Think carefully about the main point to be made when describing the emotion. For example, fear can be useful when it keeps a person from doing something dangerous.

5. Decide how to present the information. For example, a book about envy might take the form of a story in which a worm wishes it had wings like a bird.

6. Because emotions are a difficult topic, ask several readers to comment on the book and give suggestions for making it better.

FABLES BOOK

A fable is a story that teaches a lesson. The characters in a fable are almost always animals who talk like people.

DIRECTIONS:

1. Pick a topic for a fable, for example, friendship or sharing.
2. Write a sentence that explains the fable's main lesson (called "the moral"). For example, the moral for a fable about sharing could be "Sharing brings more happiness than selfishness."
3. Decide what kind of characters will star in the fable. They can be the same kind, for example, two snakes—or different kinds, for example, a cow and a dog.
4. Think up an event such as a party or trip during which characters could learn the lesson.
5. Write the story. Build the action to a moment when one or all of the characters learns the lesson.
6. End the story with the moral.

Fable Topics

chores

cleanliness

cooperation

eating

environment

fear

friendship

gifts

goals

habits (making, breaking)

helpfulness

honesty

kindness

laziness

learning

lying

manners

money (saving, spending)

nightmares

persistence

promises

reading

selfishness

sharing

television

FAMILY BOOK

Though some people belong to many groups—a band, a sports team, and so on—the first group for everyone is the family.

DIRECTIONS:
1. Choose the focus. Will the book be about one kind of family or will it describe many kinds of families? *Hint:* Some families consist of two people, for example, a child and a parent. Others may include two parents, many kids, aunts, uncles, cousins, grandparents. And some people consider pets part of the family.
2. Brainstorm a list of family activities—eating, reading together, shopping, celebrating holidays, picnicking, and so on—and use some or all of them in the book.
3. Decide how to present the information. The book could simply talk about family life. Or it could take the form of a story, for example, how two very different families move onto the same block and become good neighbors.
4. Write the book, but remember: There are many kinds of families these days. No one book can represent the experiences of every reader.

Variation: Write a book about animal families, for example, a family of robins or wolves.

FRIENDSHIP BOOK

A friendship is a great treasure. That's why so many children's books are about friends.

DIRECTIONS:
1. Brainstorm a list of friendship topics such as becoming a friend, helping a friend, overcoming differences, and making up after a fight.
2. Pick one of these friendship activities and list the steps that are involved in it. For example, to make up after a fight, friends might talk about what happened and then say they are sorry. *Hint:* For ideas, keep in mind personal friendships and friendships described in books and movies.
3. Decide how to present the information. It could be given fact by fact, for example, "The Ten Secrets of Becoming a Friend." Or ideas could be shared in a story.
4. Choose interesting characters for the book. For example, a book about how friendship can overcome differences might feature a crocodile and a chicken.

HEALTH AND SAFETY BOOK

Every year many children get sick or are injured because they did not understand the dangers around them.

DIRECTIONS:
1. Brainstorm a list of dangers that children face, for example, falling, getting burned, drowning, being hit by a car, swallowing poison, and being bitten.
2. Choose a focus for the book—either one danger or many.
3. Learn as much as possible about coping with the danger or dangers. This might involve reading books or talking to experts such as Red Cross workers or a doctor.
4. Decide how to share the information. One way is to present the facts in a list of do's and don'ts. Another way is to work the facts into a story, for example, "Sam and Sally Learn to Be Safe."
5. When writing the words, be careful to make the dangers seem really dangerous.

HOLIDAY BOOK

Every day is valuable. But some days get extra attention. A holiday book tells what makes certain days special.

DIRECTIONS:
1. Pick a day that people celebrate year after year, for example, New Year's Day or Election Day.
2. Find out when and why the day was first celebrated. Also, gather information on the activities that take place as part of the celebration.
3. Decide whether to present the information fact by fact or as a story, for example, "Mindy the Monkey Learns to Vote."
4. When writing the book, try to include ways that the reader can get involved in the celebration.

Variation: Write about a holiday celebrated in another country. Or include information about how the same holiday is celebrated here and in other countries.

Special Days

April Fool's Day

Chinese New Year

Christmas

Cinco de Mayo

Columbus Day

Easter

Election Day

Father's Day

Flag Day

Grandparents' Day

Groundhog Day

Halloween

Hanukkah

Independence Day

Labor Day

Mardi Gras

Martin Luther King Day

May Day

Memorial Day

Mother's Day

New Year's Day

Passover

President's Day

St. Patrick's Day

Thanksgiving

United Nation's Day

Valentine's Day

Veteran's Day

HOUSEHOLD HELPER BOOK

When children learn to take responsibilities for chores around the house, they not only help the family but also help themselves grow up.

DIRECTIONS:
1. Choose a chore that a young child could do—or help someone else do.
2. Break the chore into steps.
3. Decide on the form of the book. Will it simply be a how-to-do-it book, or will there be a story, for example, about someone who at first doesn't like to do the chore.
4. Create a character or several characters.
5. When writing the text, carefully explain how to do each step of the chore. Include do's and don'ts, for example—"Don't drop the telephone after saying hello."
6. Write an introduction for parents, giving hints about how they can help their child master the task described in the book.
7. Give the book a positive title—something like "I Can Make My Bed All By Myself."

Chores for Household Helpers

amuse a baby

answer the telephone

clean a room

clean up after a picnic

decorate the Christmas tree

do the dishes

fold the laundry

illustrate invitations and letters

make the bed

make visitors feel at home

prepare a simple meal

put away toys

set the table

shop at a supermarket

take care of a pet

wash the car

water the plants

work in the garden

JOB BOOK

One of the most exciting questions a child can be asked is "What do you want to be when you grow up?" In order to answer that question, children need to learn about the different jobs people do.

DIRECTIONS:
1. Pick an interesting job. It could be the kind of job people do in the neighborhood, for example, working in a fast-food restaurant. Or it could be an unusual job, for example, washing windows in a skyscraper.
2. Collect facts about the job by reading books or talking to someone who does that kind of work.
3. Decide whether to present the facts as a report or to tell them in the form of a story.
4. Describe each important part of the job. For example, a book about flying might show a pilot reading maps, inspecting the plane, talking to the control tower, and so on.
5. Write an introduction that tells why the job is important.

Note: Just about any job can be done by both men and women and by people of all races. And many jobs can be done by people with handicaps. Showing a variety of people at work will help people see the world with an open mind.

Interesting Jobs

actor

airplane pilot

armed forces member

banker

carpenter

cook

cowboy and cowgirl

doctor

electrician

engineer

entertainer

factory worker

farmer

firefighter

gardener

judge

lawyer

letter carrier

mayor

mechanic

musician

newscaster

painter

plumber

police officer

reporter

salesperson

ship's captain

teacher

truck driver

writer

MANNERS BOOK

Just as a drop of oil makes a wheel turn smoothly, good manners help people to get along with each other.

DIRECTIONS:
1. List activities in which manners play a part, for example, eating, responding to gifts, talking, going to the movies, visiting other people's houses, and so on.
2. Pick one activity and brainstorm a list of do's and don'ts. For example, a book about movie-theater manners might include tips such as "Do put your trash in the trash can" but "Don't talk while the movie is playing."
3. Decide how to present the information: either as a series of do's and don'ts or as a story, for example, about a person or animal character who learns good movie-going manners.
4. When writing the book, try to include reasons for the good behavior. For example, after writing "Don't put your feet up on the back of a chair at the movies," explain that dirt from a person's shoes may ruin someone else's clothes.

OBJECT BOOK

An important part of growing up is becoming familiar with things. This includes learning to name the parts of things and how the parts work togther.

DIRECTIONS:
1. Pick something that might be interesting to a child. It could be a household object such as a vacuum cleaner. Or it might be something more unusual, for example, an airliner.
2. List all the important parts of the object. For example, a telephone has a receiver, speaker, dial or buttons, etc.
3. Begin the book by explaining what the object is used for.
4. Describe each part of the object and how it is used.
5. Mention do's and don'ts for using the object. Include safety tips.

TREES ARE TERRIFIC
BY

Variation: Write about several things that belong together, for example, things used to eat with.

A TREE'S ROOTS DO MANY JOBS.

Objects to Write About

airplane

animal

automobile

bicycle

book

computer

dollar bill

flag

football

fruit or vegetable

kite

newspaper

pencil

refrigerator

rocket

sailboat

shoe

suspension bridge

telephone

toilet

train

tree

truck

vacuum cleaner

wheelchair

OBSERVATION BOOK

Noticing things is a skill that's important in art, science, and many, many activities throughout life.

DIRECTIONS:
1. Decide what kind of observation book to make. In one type, readers are asked to find a certain kind of thing in a picture that contains lots of other things, for example, to find all the animals in a park. In another type, readers see only part of an object through a hole cut in the page, for example, stripes from the side of a zebra. Readers then try to guess what the hidden thing is.
2. Brainstorm a list of things to include.
3. Illustrate each page. *Hint:* Little kids love looking for itty-bitty things that are almost too tiny to see.
4. Add words that tell the readers what to do.

OPPOSITES BOOK

Up/down. In/out. Hot/_____. To fill in that last blank—and to come up with other word opposites—a person has to think.

DIRECTIONS:

1. Brainstorm a list of pairs that are opposites. Think about size (giant/midget), texture (smooth/rough), speed (fast/slow), difficulty (easy/hard), and so on.

2. Decide how to format the book. One way is to present the opposites on the same page. Another way is to make the book into a kind of guessing game—put one word on the right-hand page and the opposite on the next page, so the reader gets to guess before seeing the answer.

3. After writing and illustrating the book, add an introduction that explains opposites and why it's important to learn about them.

PARTICIPATION BOOK

Most books ask readers only to think or imagine. But a participation book really involves the reader.

DIRECTIONS:
1. Brainstorm activities that children can do while reading a book or while being read to. Examples include clapping, giggling, humming, pointing to something in the book, smacking their lips, blinking, or imitating sounds from nature such as the wind or an animal.
2. Decide whether to describe the actions separately or to make them part of a story.
3. Begin the book by telling the reader to get ready to do different actions.
4. After completing the text, try the activities out to make sure they work.

Variation: Write a play that young readers could act out as someone reads the words. Include a section that explains how to make masks and costumes for the play.

PLACE BOOK

People often like to read about faraway countries such as Australia. But nearby places can be just as interesting.

DIRECTIONS:
1. Choose a place that young children often visit or might visit, for example, the supermarket.
2. List all the important parts of the place. *Hint:* If possible, go there and take notes firsthand.
3. Write a page or two about each part of the place.
4. Add an introduction that explains why the place is worth knowing about.
5. Include a map that shows all parts of the place.

Variation: Write about a future place, for example, about what a home will look like a hundred years from now.

Places to Write About

airport

bank

church or synagogue

circus

dentist's office

department store

doctor's office

farm

fire station

gas station

hospital

house

library

movie theater

museum

newspaper

playground

police station

post office

publishing company

shopping mall

skyscraper

supermarket

television station

train station

veterinarian's office

zoo

PROBLEM-SOLVING BOOK

Children, like adults, can sometimes use help dealing with difficulties.

DIRECTIONS:

1. Pick a problem that affects children. It might be something that almost all kids have to face, for example, nightmares. Or it might be something that only some kids have to deal with, for example, moving to a new home.

2. Figure out one or more ways for handling the problem. This might require reading books or talking with experts.

3. Decide how to present the information. It could be done in a general way, for example, "Lots of people are afraid of the dark." Or the ideas could be presented in a story, for example, "Joanne and the Dark Closet."

4. When writing the story, think about how a child would look at the problem. *Hint:* What might seem silly to a bigger kid or grown-up might be very scary to a four-year-old.

Problems Children May Have

arguing

begging for things

being ignored

boredom

bragging

breaking a promise

breaking something valuable

bullying or being bullied

carelessness

crying

disobedience

envy

fear of
    animals
    the babysitter
    being different
    the dark
    the doctor
    growing up
    thunder and lightning
    water

fighting

forgetfulness

getting dirty

getting lost

greediness

having a bad day

lateness

loneliness

losing things

lying

messiness

milk spilling

misunderstanding

moving to a new home

nightmares

not listening

prejudice

running away

screaming

shyness

stealing

talking to strangers

talking too much

upset stomach

worrying

REPETITIVE STORY

Many children's stories grow from a single action that happens over and over with small changes. One of the most famous examples is *The Runaway Bunny*. In that story, a little bunny tells its mother all the different ways it plans to run away. But every time the mother has a plan to find the bunny.

DIRECTIONS:
1. Make a list of actions that children do, for example, getting dressed or asking questions.
2. Pick one of the actions and brainstorm many variations on it. For example, a child could get dressed for the beach, the snow, the rain, and so on. Or a child could forget to put away clothes, toys, books, food, and so on.
3. Think up an important word or phrase that will be repeated throughout the book, for example:

Why do _____?
I might _____.
Where is _____?
It fell down.
Can I have _____?

4. Write the story, being sure to repeat the word or phrase on almost every page.

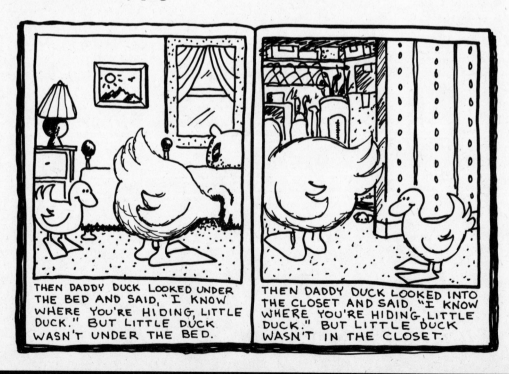

THEN DADDY DUCK LOOKED UNDER THE BED AND SAID, "I KNOW WHERE YOU'RE HIDING, LITTLE DUCK." BUT LITTLE DUCK WASN'T UNDER THE BED.

THEN DADDY DUCK LOOKED INTO THE CLOSET AND SAID, "I KNOW WHERE YOU'RE HIDING, LITTLE DUCK." BUT LITTLE DUCK WASN'T IN THE CLOSET.

Repeatable Activities

bathing

building with blocks

cooking

dreaming

eating

imagining different places

listening to a music box

looking out the window

painting

playing hide and go seek

pretending to read a book

riding a tricycle

rocking on a rocking horse

shopping in the supermarket

singing

talking on the telephone

walking the dog

watering a plant or garden

RIDDLE BOOK

What's a question that makes people think hard and then smile even if they can't figure out the answer? If you guessed "riddle," you guessed right.

DIRECTIONS:
1. Brainstorm a list of people, places, and things that children will know about.
2. Write three or four clues that might help someone guess what each thing is. Sometimes it's fun to write the clues as if the thing can talk:
> I'm cold but I don't feel it.
> I can't swim but I float.
> If you drop me in water, I'll disappear.

End the list of clues with a question, for example:
> What am I?

3. Put the clues in order from least helpful to most helpful.
4. When putting the riddle book together, print the clues on the right-hand page and the answer on the back.

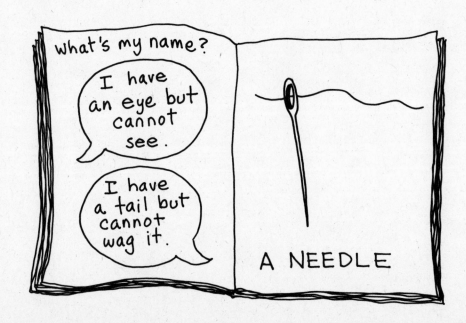

Subjects to Write Riddles About

bathtub

bicycle

book

butterfly

car

ceiling

cloud

dream

floor

house

moon

morning

night

pets

rain

school

seasons

sidewalk

snow

stop sign

sun

telephone

television

wind

SCIENCE BOOK

Science isn't a subject just for adults. Anyone who looks closely at things and actions is a scientist. And that includes even very young children.

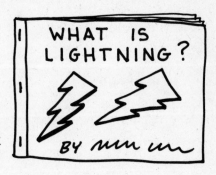

DIRECTIONS:
1. Pick a science topic—anything from ants to wind.
2. Brainstorm activities readers can do in order to learn more about the topic. For example, a book about water might ask readers to put water into a freezer to see what happens to it. A book about how rockets work could include a simple experiment with a balloon.
3. Gather information—both facts and how-to's for activities—by reading books and talking with experts.
4. Decide whether to present the ideas in a regular science book format, for example, "Let's Study Leaves"— or as a story, for example, "Terry Learns About Turtles."
5. When writing the book, include plenty of pictures that help readers know what to look for and do.

Variation: Write a science quiz book. For example, one page could show a kite flying and could ask what keeps a kite up in the air. The following page could give the answer.

SHAPE AND SIZE BOOK

Shape and size are important to painters, shoppers, cooks, scientists, and others who deal with things. And that's just about everybody—including children.

DIRECTIONS:
1. List the main topics the book will cover. For example, will it simply help readers understand the difference between big and little? Or will it try to explain that size is relative? For example, a pickup truck may be called "big" when compared with a child but "small" when compared with a tractor trailer.
2. Decide how to present the information. It could be done as a fact book or as a storybook—"Sally Sees Circles."
3. Use plenty of pictures. These can be simple figures or they can be objects in the real world, for example, bicycle wheels that stand for circles.
4. Include an introduction that explains why it's important to learn about shape and size.

Shape and Size Words

Shape Words
ball (sphere)
box (cube)
center
cone
corner
cube
curve
dot
egg shaped (ellipse)
flat
inside
line
narrow
oblong
outside
round
side
square
straight
thick
triangular

Size Words
big/bigger
equal
heavy/heavier
length
less than
light/lighter
little/tiny
long/longer
more than
same as
short/shorter
small/smaller
volume
weight
wide/wider
width

SPATIAL RELATIONS BOOK

Up, down, all around—children need to know "where in the world" things are.

DIRECTIONS:

1. Brainstorm a list of location words such as *above, below, under, over, in, out, near, before, after,* and *on.*
2. Decide how to teach about these words. One way is to explain them one at a time. Another is to think up a story in which one or several characters—people or animals—move around in space.
3. Write the book. Include pictures that help get across the different location ideas.

Variation: Figure out a way to get the reader actively involved in the book. For example, the words might ask the reader to touch an object *on* the table or *in* the box.

STORYBOOK

A storybook can open the imagination while teaching important lessons about life.

DIRECTIONS:

1. In a sentence or two, describe the main characters who will be in the story. Characters can be people. Or they can be animals or things that act like people. *Hint:* Many stories are exciting because they include villains who cause trouble for other people. An example is the Big Bad Wolf. However, some stories that have no villains are still very interesting because the main characters have to struggle with exciting things like storms or fears.

2. In a sentence or two, describe the big problem that the main character or characters must deal with. Examples of problems are:
   - Trying to win a race
   - Trying to find something that's been lost
   - Trying to help someone who is in danger
   - Trying to overcome a bad person
   - Trying to overcome a fear

3. In a sentence or two, explain what will happen at the end of the story.

4. Write a "story outline" that lists actions that might take place as the main character or characters struggle to solve the problem.

5. Write a few lines describing each important place in the book.

6. Using the outline, write the story in short chunks of action. Each will take a page or two in the book. After writing each chunk, describe a picture that will go with the words.

7. Create the pictures.

8. Check the words to make sure they don't simply say what the pictures show. If necessary, change the words or the pictures.

9. Give the story a title that could not be used with any other storybook.

Story Characters Found in Picture Books

animals

brothers

children

clowns

dinosaurs

elves

fairies

friends

giants

grandparents

kings

magicians

mean people

monsters

parents

princes

princesses

queens

scarecrows

selfish people

silly people

sisters

strangers

teachers

toys

trolls

troublemakers

wind

wise people

witches

TIME BOOK

The smartest scientists in the world aren't sure what time *is*. But a book can help explain what clocks and calendars are all about.

DIRECTIONS:
1. Choose a time topic to explain, for example, hour, day, week, month, season, year, tomorrow, or clock.
2. Brainstorm words that relate to the topic. For example, a book that tries to explain the idea of "day" will probably include the words hour, clock, morning, evening, and so on.
3. Decide how to get across the information. A time book might simply present facts. Or it might contain characters whose actions help teach the lesson, for example, children who are always late to school because they don't understand what it means to be "on time."

WORDLESS BOOK

There are no words in a wordless book, but words go into its making.

DIRECTIONS:

1. Get an idea for an activity or a story—especially one that has lots of action.
2. Write an outline that describes each action that will appear in the book. Use plenty of details.
3. Draw pictures that show the actions described in the outline—or work with an artist who will draw the pictures.
4. Test the book to see if "readers" can follow the action. Ask them to tell the story out loud as they look at the pictures. Wherever these readers get confused, be prepared to change a picture or add a new one that makes the book clearer.

RESOURCES

Becoming a Picture Book Author in Twelve Easy Steps

Like most forms of writing, a picture book tells a story or presents facts. But there's a big difference: the art in a picture book is as important as the words. For the book to be good, the words and the pictures must work together.

The following steps are meant to help authors create picture books worth reading and looking at.

STEP 1. GETTING AN IDEA

Every book starts with an idea, something that interests the writer. It could be what happens to a made-up character, for example, a rock that turns into a person. Or it could be a lesson about something real, for example, how the telephone works.

Ideas are everywhere. Sometimes an idea comes while the writer is doing something ordinary such as walking down the street, reading, talking to someone, or taking a bath. But an idea can also happen when a person is excited, upset, or even asleep.

Hint: Because ideas are easy to forget, many writers store them in notebooks for use later on.

STEP 2. GROWING AN IDEA

An idea is just a beginning. The more a writer thinks about the subject, the more there will be to put into the book.

Sometimes a writer needs to learn more about the subject. This research can be done by reading what other writers have written, by talking to people who know about the subject, or by using one or more of the five senses.

Look for unusual facts that will surprise readers. All kids know that cows go "moo," but most will be amazed to learn that a cow can weigh nearly as much as a car.

STEP 3. PLANNING THE PAGES

Before writing a book, it's helpful to decide what it will look like and even to create a few sample pages.

Picture books can be big, little, or in between. They can be vertical (tall) or horizontal (wide). Sometimes, but not too often, one will even take on the shape of its subject, for example, an Easter egg book might look like an egg.

Even more unusual are "special format" books. These can include pages with:

- Movable parts, for example, a pull-tab used to slide a worm in and out of the ground, or flaps that let windows and doors open and close
- Cutouts, for example, a keyhole through which readers can peek at the next scene
- Pop-up figures, for example, a flower that becomes a three-dimensional object when the book is opened

Planning also includes deciding where the pictures and words will go. Usually, one or two patterns will be followed throughout the book, for example, a picture on one page and words on the next. Or words under each picture.

Hint: For more ideas about how to create eye-pleasing pages, read lots of picture books.

STEP 4. OUTLINING THE BOOK

With other kinds of books, writers are usually free to fill as many pages as needed to deal with their subjects. But this is not the case when writing picture books. Most picture books have between 24 and 32 pages. And each page may have only one or a few sentences. So, every word must be carefully chosen.

One way to be sure that everything will fit is to make a "dummy" (practice book) that has the same size and number of pages as the finished book will have. When making the dummy, be sure to include the "front matter" found in almost every picture book:

- Title page, which repeats the cover information and also names the publisher

THIS BOOK IS FOR MY CAT FLUTTER TAIL.

COPYRIGHT 1991 BY SANDY OPERFELT

- Dedication page, which names someone whom the author admires or wants to thank:
     This book is for my sister, Sharon.
  The dedication page also includes a copyright notice that tells when the book was published:
     Copyright 1991 by Irwin Hill
- Author page, which gives a few interesting facts about the author and the illustrator (some people prefer placing this page at the end of a book)

STEP 5. WRITING THE BOOK

A picture book manuscript uses words in two ways. First, there are words that will appear in the finished book. While the main goal is to be clear, the writer may add special touches such as rhyme or repetition. Second, the manuscript includes words that describe the art that will go into the book.

For example, suppose someone is writing a book about Janey and Carl, two children who are learning to use a magnifying glass. The manuscript may look like this:

page 14

> "Now, let's look at this
> little ant," said Janey.
>
> "What do you see?" asked Carl.
>
> Art: Show an ant as it would look through a
> magnifying glass.

Another way to prepare the manuscript is to divide the page up and down. The words that will go into the finished book will be on the left side. The words that tell the artist what to do go on the right.

	Words in Book	Art
page 14	"Now, let's look at this little ant," said Janey. "What do you see?" asked Carl.	Show an ant as it would look through a magnifying glass.

STEP 6. PREPARING THE ILLUSTRATIONS

Picture books can have many kinds of art:

- Drawings: The writer or another person creates the pictures using colored pencils, ink, finger paints, felt-tip markers, crayons, watercolors, or a computer. The ideas for the drawings come from the manuscript. It's important, of course, to plan the size of each drawing before creating it. *Hint:* To keep pencil drawings from smearing, spray them with a fixative before pasting them into the finished book.

- Photographs: The writer or someone else takes photos of people, places, or things. These pictures are often used for fact books, for example, one about shadows or pets. Photographs of puppets, dolls, or people in costumes can also be used to tell stories.

- Objects: Yarn, ribbon, foil, paper clips, stickers, petals, and other things can be glued or taped into place to illustrate stories or fact books.

- Other media: Rubbings, paper collages, prints (made with fingers, potato stamps, and rubber stamps) can be used alone or mixed to create imaginative pictures.

STEP 7. LETTERING OR TYPING THE TEXT

After reading over and correcting the words, a writer should neatly letter or type the text onto clean paper. A computer setup can be used to create a variety of type sizes and shapes.

Most often, white paper is used for book pages, but in some cases colored sheets can add interest.

STEP 8. COMBINING THE WORDS AND THE ART

The usual method is to attach the art onto pages that already contain the typed or hand-lettered words. Before using glue or paste, make sure the art is in the right position. *Hint:* Because paste can leave lumps, many picture book makers recommend using glue sticks.

Teddy bear needed a friend.

STEP 9. CREATING THE COVER, JACKET, AND FRONT MATTER

The cover should have an interesting title, the author's name, the artist's name (if different from the author), and an eye-catching picture—which could be a copy of a picture used inside the book. The cover should be made of heavy cardboard and, for long wear, should be laminated.

A book jacket, which protects the book, is made from one large sheet of paper and consists of the following parts:

- Front panel, which resembles the book's front cover
- Back panel, which can have a picture from the book
- Front flap, which tells what the book is about
- Back flap, which tells about the author and artist
- Spine, which gives the title and author

For a realistic, shiny look, laminate the book jacket or cover it with a sheet of clear shelf paper.

STEP 10. BINDING THE PAGES

If more than one copy of the book is desired, duplicate the pages before binding them. Many photocopy machines make it easy to print pages back and front, thus increasing the authentic look of the book.

Of the many ways to bind pages into a finished book, three classic methods are:

- Stapling—easy and inexpensive. To improve the appearance, cover the staples with tape.
- Ring or ribbon binding—nearly as easy as stapling and can be a plus if books that lay flat are wanted.
- Stitching—classy and long-lasting, but it does require a bit of effort. For details, see *Book Factory* (Monday Morning Books, 1988).

Hint: For extra strength, place the same kind of cardboard used for the cover at the back of the book.

STEP 11. SHARING THE BOOK

A book isn't finished until it's read. One way to share a picture book is to read it aloud to children. This can be done at school, at a library story hour, or at home.

Of course, the author doesn't have to be there in person. A copy of the finished book can be donated to the school or town library. To make sure people ask for it, send a copy to the local newspaper's book reviewer.

Still another way to share a picture book is to enter it in a young authors' festival. For information, contact the county office of education or the local reading association.

Finally, picture books make wonderful gifts.

STEP 12. EVALUATING THE BOOK

To become a better writer, it's a good idea to think about a book after it's finished. Ask questions such as "What's good about this book?" and "What would have made it even better?"

Another way to evaluate a book is to watch what happens when it's read aloud. Do the listeners look interested? Do they laugh in the right places? Do they ask good questions?

If they fall asleep, that's not a good sign . . . unless the picture book is a bedtime story.

Model Picture Books

Children should read lots of examples (models) of the kind of picture books they will be writing themselves. Creativity comes when they add their own personal ideas, experiences, observations, interpretations, and so on. (For an in-depth treatment of using models, see *Recipes for Writing*, Addison-Wesley, 1989.)

Luckily, there is no shortage of models when it comes to picture books. A recent index lists over 14,000 titles in print. The following is a list of recommended picture books.

ACTIVITY BOOKS
HICKORY STICK RAG by Clyde Watson
IN OUR HOUSE by Anne Rockwell
PANCAKES FOR BREAKFAST by Tomie de Paola
PETUNIA TAKES A TRIP by Roger Duvoisin
WHAT'S GOOD FOR A SIX-YEAR-OLD by William Cole

ADD-ON BOOKS
BROWN BEAR, BROWN BEAR, WHAT DO YOU SEE? by
    Bill Martin, Jr.
BUZZ, BUZZ, BUZZ by Byron Barton
CAT GOES FIDDLE-I-FEE by Paul Galdone
THE GINGERBREAD BOY by Paul Galdone
THE HOUSE THAT JACK BUILT by Seymour Chwast
I KNOW AN OLD LADY by Rose Bonne
THE LITTLE RED HEN by Margot Zemach
MILLIONS OF CATS by Wanda Gag
MR. GUMPY'S OUTING by John Burningham
ONE FINE DAY by Nonny Hogrogian

ALPHABET BOOKS
A APPLE PIE by Kate Greenaway
ABC BUNNY by Wanda Gag
ALFRED'S ALPHABET WALK by Victoria Chess
ALLIGATOR ARRIVED WITH APPLES by Crescent
    Dragonwagon
ALLIGATORS ALL AROUND by Maurice Sendak
ANIMALS A TO Z by David McPhail
ASHANTI TO ZULU by Margaret Musgrove
JOHN BURNINGHAM'S ABC by John Burningham
SLEEPY ABC by Margaret Wise Brown
THE Z WAS ZAPPED by Chris Van Allsburg

ANIMAL FACT BOOKS
KOKO'S KITTEN by Francine Patterson
NIGHT ANIMALS by Millicent E. Selsam
PREHISTORIC ANIMALS by Gail Gibbons
THE YEAR AT MAPLE HILL FARM by Alice Provensen

ANIMAL STORYBOOKS
ANIMALS SHOULD DEFINITELY NOT WEAR CLOTHING
    by Judi Barrett
BLACKBOARD BEAR by Martha Alexander
THE CHURCH MOUSE by Graham Oakley
CLAUDE THE DOG by Dick Gackenbach
HENNY PENNY by Paul Galdone
LEO THE LATE BLOOMER by Robert Kraus
LITTLE BEAR by Else Holmelund Minarik
LITTLE FOX GOES TO THE END OF THE WORLD by
    Ann Tompert
PETUNIA by Roger Duvoisin
SYLVESTER AND THE MAGIC PEBBLE by William Steig
THE TALE OF PETER RABBIT by Beatrix Potter
WHO'S IN RABBIT'S HOUSE? by Virginia Aardema

BABY BOOKS
THE BABY'S GOOD MORNING BOOK by Kay Chorao
BIG BROTHER by Robert Kraus
EVERETT ANDERSON'S NINE MONTH LONG by Lucille
    Clifton
NOBODY ASKED ME IF I WANTED A BABY SISTER by
    Martha Alexander
PEEK-A-BOO! by Janet Ahlberg
WELCOME, LITTLE BABY by Aliki
WHERE'S THE BABY? by Pat Hutchins

BEDTIME STORYBOOKS
CLOSE YOUR EYES by Jean Marzollo
GOOD NIGHT, GOOD MORNING by Helen Oxenbury
GOODNIGHT HORSEY by Frank Asch
GOODNIGHT MOON by Margaret Wise Brown
I HEAR A NOISE by Diane Goode

COLOR BOOKS
A COLOR OF HIS OWN by Leo Lionni
MR. RABBIT AND THE LOVELY PRESENT by Charlotte
     Zolotow
RED LIGHT, GREEN LIGHT by Margaret Wise Brown
YELLOW, YELLOW by Frank Asch

COUNTING BOOKS
BABAR'S COUNTING BOOK by Laurent de Brunhoff
FIVE DOWN by John Burningham
MOJO MEANS ONE by Muriel Feelings
ONE WAS JOHNNY by Maurice Sendak
SO MANY CATS by Beatrice Schenk de Regniers
TEN, NINE, EIGHT by Molly Bang

EMOTIONS BOOKS
ALEXANDER AND THE WINDUP MOUSE by Leo Lionni
I WAS SO MAD! by Norma Simon
NOEL THE COWARD by Robert Kraus
THE QUARRELING BOOK by Charlotte Zolotow
ROTTEN RALPH'S ROTTEN CHRISTMAS by Jack Gantos
TO HILDA FOR HELPING by Margot Zemach

FABLES
AESOP'S FABLES by Alice and Martin Provensen
FABLES by Arnold Lobel
THE HARE AND THE TORTOISE by Paul Galdone
SEVEN FABLES FROM AESOP by Robert W. Alley

FAMILY BOOKS
BLUEBERRIES FOR SAL by Robert McCloskey
COULD BE WORSE! by James Stevenson
MY BROTHER FINE WITH ME by Lucille Clifton
THE TERRIBLE THING THAT HAPPENED AT OUR
     HOUSE by Marge Blaine
WILLIAM'S DOLL by Charlotte Zolotow
WRETCHED RACHEL by Diane Paterson

FRIENDSHIP BOOKS
BEST FRIENDS by Steven Kellogg
DO YOU WANT TO BE MY FRIEND? by Eric Carle
GEORGE AND MARTHA by James Marshall
IRA SLEEPS OVER by Bernard Waber
NICE NEW NEIGHBORS by Franz Brandenberg

HEALTH AND SAFETY BOOKS
ALLIGATOR'S TOOTHACHE by Diane de Groat
HATTIE BE QUIET, HATTIE BE GOOD by Dick
    Gackenbach
LEOPARD IS SICK by Giulio Maestro
RED LIGHT, GREEN LIGHT by Margaret Wise Brown
TRY IT AGAIN SAM by Judith Viorst
YUMMERS by James Marshall

HOLIDAY BOOKS
A PICTURE BOOK OF JEWISH HOLIDAYS by David
    Adler
ARTHUR'S APRIL FOOL by Marc Brown
ARTHUR'S CHRISTMAS COOKIES by Lillian Hoban
FATHER CHRISTMAS by Raymond Briggs
HAPPY VALENTINE'S DAY, EMMA by James Stevenson
HOW THE GRINCH STOLE CHRISTMAS by Dr. Seuss
THE SILVER CHRISTMAS TREE by Pat Hutchins

JOB BOOKS
AN ACTOR and A WRITER by M.F. Goffstein
MIKE MULLIGAN AND HIS STEAM SHOVEL
    by Virginia Lee Burton
MOTHERS CAN DO ANYTHING by Joe Lasker
WALTER THE BAKER by Eric Carle

OPPOSITES BOOKS
FAST-SLOW, HIGH-LOW by Peter Spier
PUSH-PULL, EMPTY-FULL by Tana Hoban
WHAT THE MOON SAW by Brian Wildsmith

PROBLEM-SOLVING BOOKS
BABAR LOSES HIS CROWN by Laurent de Brunhoff
THE CAR TRIP by Helen Oxenbury
I'M TAGGARTY TOAD by Peter Pavey
KEEP YOUR MOUTH CLOSED DEAR by Aliki
LOUDMOUTH GEORGE AND THE SIXTH GRADE
    BULLY by Nancy Carlson
MINE'S THE BEST by Crosby Bonsall
WHAT DID YOU BRING ME? by Karla Kuskin

REPETITIVE BOOKS
GREEN EGGS AND HAM by Dr. Seuss
THE GROUCHY LADYBUG by Eric Carle
IF YOU GIVE A MOUSE A COOKIE by Laura Joffe
    Numeroff
MILLIONS OF CATS by Wanda Gag
POOR ESME by Victoria Chess
RUNAWAY BUNNY by Margaret Wise Brown
TIKKI TIKKI TEMBO by Arlene Mosel

SHAPES BOOKS
PEZZETTINO by Leo Lionni
THE SHAPE OF ME AND OTHER STUFF by Dr. Seuss
SHAPES, SHAPES, SHAPES by Tana Hoban

SPECIAL FORMAT BOOKS
THE ADVENTURES OF PADDY PORK by John Goodall
JOSEPH HAD A LITTLE OVERCOAT by Simms Taback
THE MOST AMAZING HIDE-AND-SEEK ALPHABET
    BOOK by Robert Crowther
THE VERY HUNGRY CATERPILLAR by Eric Carle

TIME BOOKS
AROUND THE CLOCK WITH HARRIET by Betsy Maestro
BEAR CHILD'S BOOK OF HOURS by Anne Rockwell
CLOCKS AND MORE CLOCKS by Pat Hutchins
TIME by Jan Pienkowski

WORDLESS BOOKS
AH CHOO! by Mercer Mayer
THE EGG BOOK by Jack Kent
NOAH'S ARK by Peter Spier
THE SURPRISE PICNIC by John Goodall